GET YOUR BOOK PUBLISHED

ON KINDLE AMAZON

By

Sandratana Camille

Contact

Sandratana Camille

Marist International University College

Marist Lane, Karen, Nairobi Kenya

Mail:csandratana@yahoo.fr

Tel: +254 73 444 1620

Acknowledgement

To all of my friends who helped me and supported me in different ways of writing this work. You helped me to come up with this book that I could never have done without your encouragement.

Special thanks to Mercy for her advice and support related to business and commerce.

About the Author

Sandratana Camille was born and grew up in the area of Ihazolava, Ambatolampy Madagascar. During his stay in Nairobi Kenya in 1988 to 1991, he developed the passion of computer learning that would be performed by his further training in computer programming. It was by his returning back to Nairobi again in 2005 that brings him to be the Senior ICT Officer of Marist International University College in Kenya.

Sandratana Camille has been a freelance ICT-Technology profession for more than 10 years. His IT credits include: Sandratana Camille Software: 'UsbCleaner' and 'Petty Cash Accounting'. In addition to his skills in programming, he has also great knowledge of HTML and PHP script programs that enable him to create websites for different organizations and e-commerce websites for online stores.

This book *"Get Your Book Published on Kindle Amazon"* opens the way with the detailed guide for writers who want to self-publish their work. While traditional publishing a book has never been done without a high cost, this book of Sandratana Camille shows you other ways. It brings you to discover the power of digital media, which has revolutionized the publishing business to favor writers, including new authors. It empowers you with practical skills on editing your book with cover design to be published on Amazon. By reading this book, you also get marketing advice to write your book. Do you want to publish your book without high cost? You can do yourself!

TABLE OF CONTENTS

INTRODUCTION

On December 2011, Amazon revolutionized the digital book industry with their introduction to KDP Select service. KDP (Kindle Direct Publishing) helps authors and publishers publish their digital book completely free on the Kindle platform which is essentially aimed at the promotion of new writers to become self-published authors. Amazon is now granting access to powerful marketing tools. This unique approach was taken by Amazon as a way of helping unknown authors to succeed in the publication of their eBook. KDP or Kindle Direct Publishing is an opportunity for new authors to self-publish eBooks.

However, it requires the author to accept his Kindle eBook to be distributed exclusively on Amazon for 90 days for free. From the total of 90 days, up to 5 days are given to access the promotional tool for marketing eBooks using the Amazon platform. When this period of 90 days is granted, the author can promote the eBook for free for up to five days by allowing Amazon Prime members to make free daily borrowing through a loan program service called "Kindle Owners' Lending Library". Amazon Prime is a special membership that charges a single annual fee. However, you may sign up for a trial and reap all of the benefits that come with the membership. Prime members are able to borrow one eBook per month and read them on their computer, kindle or smart phone.

Authors, entering in the KDP Select program will earn a share from the fund that Amazon offers every time your eBook is borrowed in Kindle Owners' Lending Library. The bonus was $2.2 million to cover December 2012-February 2013, which is an amount added to the monthly regular fund. It is to compensate the authors for giving free loans to Prime members. Authors can take advantage of all of these benefits and gain new audiences as well as the free "digitally" published book is set available for Amazon Prime members. This potential marketing is expected to generate revenue right away due to the promotion. As an author, it can be good to offer at least one eBook in the KDP and take the opportunity to get readers. It promotes your visibility and helps you discover more new readers.

Taking a chance and having your book published in the largest internet retailer can be profitable and good for recognition. Why would anyone not take a chance and decide to get their content and knowledge published on Amazon? It is simple and fast. This book will show and breakdown every single step necessary to become a self-published author on Amazon's Kindle Platform. After reading this book, you should be able to self-publish your own Kindle eBook content fast and easy on Amazon. You will get from this valuable source the information you need to know how to format your eBook using the technical steps for publishing. In short, you will get the techniques needed in order to publish your first Kindle eBook. You will also be able to make your creativity known in the biggest digital book market in the world.

You will learn the fundamental skills to become the self-published author on Amazon. At first sight, the steps seem to be complex, but with the information which will be brought to you, the method becomes a simple action to be completed. This book is divided into four major categories that cover the overall process:

1. Understanding the Amazon Self-Published Author.

2. Writing and copyrighting information.

3. Formatting and publishing your eBook.

4. Promoting your first eBook.

In this book, useful tips to help you to become a self-published author are developed in progressive steps. Some added values on this guide include, editing your first content, adding visuals and graphics to your eBook, designing high quality covers for your eBook, understanding the concept of pricing digital goods, using royalties for a better book promotions, providing detailed information on other places to sell your eBook and knowing other services dealing with self-publishing.

Format of eBooks can be read and reviewed with online reading in (HTML) form, with Kindle in (Mobi) form, with iPad, Nook, iBooks, Adobe Digital Editions, Kobo and Sony Reader in (ePub) form, with PC in (PDF, RTF) file, and there are also other readers devices.

After creating useful eBook content, how do you let the audience know that your eBook even exists? The discovery of internet libraries and digital book stores are another challenge self-published authors must tackle. Successful self-published eBook author Valerie Estelle Frankel shares some tips on how to market and create buzz regarding eBook[1]. Using social media giants such as Facebook, Ebay and Twitter, Valerie Estelle was able to find her audience and market her books to them. In your turn, you should be ready to create press releases, which build awareness of your product. The use of social media to market your eBook is among the powerful tools you can take note. The cover graphic design to outsource your book contributes a great part in promoting your book. These will result in more readers and more commercially successful eBooks.

How to self-publish your Kindle eBooks on the Amazon website? This is the main topic of this book. Take the opportunity to publish your book on the largest sites on the web. Do you want to get your book published on Amazon? Learn from this reading how to format your book and publish it yourself.

CHAPTER I

1. - Understanding the Amazon Self-Published Author

1.1 - The Amazon free publishing tools

Amazon has created one of the most effective marketing strategies that allow unknown authors to publish and build publicity. Nevertheless some authors may not know and do not discover yet this opportunity. Kindle books are more than a "platform book", they are available in smart phones (through amazon apps), computers, and tablets. This wide reach is just one of the reasons publishers should not let this opportunity pass away.

The Amazon's Free-Play program allows new authors to publish eBooks and give them for free. This promotional tool allows the book to receive thousands of downloads and go up in popularity across the amazon store. If the book is good, and it receives a lot of downloads and high rating, Amazon will begin to rank the book in the most popular categories. Much like Apple's top apps download list, as your book gains more popularity, the more exposure it will gain. Once your eBook has reached the top, you can stop the free eBook give away promotion and turn it into a paid eBook. When your eBook has become a premium in the top list, you can expect to generate more sales.

In a nutshell, the concept revolves around promotional marketing. By giving away free eBook samples, you can expect blogs promoting your eBook, reviews, word of mouth, and product buzz. All of these elements in its essence are signs of a successful marketing campaign. Giving away some of your material for free also helps build a loyal fan base. The same readers are likely to buy from you if they enjoy your free promotion.

"Free" material can be one of the greatest driving forces when it comes to sales in the eBook marketplace. If you have written an eBook series, offering a free sample of one single eBook can boost sales of the other eBooks in the series tremendously. Readers who enjoyed your content are willingly to pay more in order to get more quality writing.

1.2 - Does free sample promotional marketing work for new authors?

The following results are the product of a survey published by forbes.com[2] and conducted with the help of 74 published kindle authors. The survey took place in January through April 2012.

Average of 17 book reviews was added per book during the period the book was free. Books that took part of the survey had an average price of $2.99 during their paid status. Free book promotion was lasted 2 days in average. The number of downloads during the promotions average at 4000. The weekly amount of books sold prior to free promotion averaged at 5. The weekly amount of books sold after promotions averaged at 49. An 87 percent of the 74 authors who took part of this experiment say they are likely to conduct this marketing strategy again.

In order to offer more incentives to authors to agree to take part of their lending program, Amazon designates, in December 2012, a monthly pool of 500,000 dollars that will be distributed among the authors evenly depending on the amount of times their books were downloaded. An example on how, after a month, this incentive works would be if the total amount of downloads of your eBooks equates to a total of 1.5 percent of the total downloads in the lending program. You will receive 1.5 percent of the total pot or 7,500 dollars.

As documented in this example, some of the positives of this program are the earning potential some authors are able to produce. However, Amazon's book lending program also comes with strict terms and conditions. While your books take part of the lending program, you become virtually powerless over the rights of the book. Amazon's terms and conditions indicate that you may not advertise, sell or even promote your book for sale in any other platform such as Barnes and Noble, Apple or Kobo.

This means that Amazon has the rights of exclusivity of your book during this period. In essence, it is important to be aware of the pros and cons of the program before ever enrolling in it. If you decide to remove your books from the three months program, you may regain your book rights again and distribute the book as you please. However, removing your books before due time (3 months) can cause you to lose earnings you might have accumulated, or even get banned from the program. Naturally, once your three months period ends you may decide whether or not you wish your books to keep participating in the program. If you do not choose anything, Amazon automatically renews your contract and your books take part of the lending course for another three months.

1.3 - The effect of Amazon's KDP Program on authors

The program obligates authors who have multiple digital distribution channels to end partnerships for the sake complying with Amazon's regulations. Joining the program can be counter-productive to established authors who have acquired ranks and recognition in other eBook platforms. By entering Amazon's program, authors un-diversify their income streams and thus increase the risk of "putting all eggs in one basket".

1.4 - The effect of Amazon's KDP Program on competitors

The program takes content available from other competitors by restricting authors to publish content on their market place. Popular authors may decide to stop working with a competitor in order to seek higher earnings with amazon. The program increases the amount of customers who buy from amazon as they acquire unique content boosted from the promotion.

1.5 - How the KDP has affected the Publishing Industry?

Authors who did not have the recognition to drive sales were left off side of the eBook market. When Amazon managed to focus the eBook market into a single platform, the eBook industries, as well as the self-published author community, were affected greatly. Here are just some of the effects Amazon has had over the first KDP launching year.

KDP allows authors to self-publish for no cost. This has led to over 500 books reaching the top 100 Kindle book's list during the first year of KDP Select Program. It means, this raise up of top list has happened from December 2011 to December 2012. Authors who publish exclusively with KDP are estimated to earn from the 7 million dollars, an amount invested by Amazon during the first year launching to run the KDP lending global program. This is without counting, royalties and other paid sales. In total, books downloaded from the lending program, the free category as well as paid books went to the amount of over 200 million downloads.

1.6 - Short closer look at Amazon's success

Being one of the fortune 500 companies, Amazon is influential in our daily lives. Amazon began operating in 1995 as a web based, book Retailer Company based in Seattle. As the company began to gain momentum and power it expanded into different departments, most of them e-commerce related. Today, Amazon sells millions of items in a huge range of categories. Items can be sold through amazon by companies or by individuals. From movies, electronics, digital products to music and books; all of these items represent some of Amazon's most successful products. Aside from products, Amazon's business infrastructure has allowed it to expand in the service industry. Some of Amazon's most profitable and growing service is cloud storage. Cloud storage allows individuals to store digital files in a third party (amazon's) server and access it anytime anywhere. Cloud storage is able to power many businesses enterprises and business operations that work closely with Amazon.

Amazon's cloud leads the way in eBook reader by bringing the first known device, the Kindle. The Kindle was a high resolution, black and white electronic device that accesses Amazon's eBook store and allows customers to purchase electronic books and directly read them. The original Kindle was launched in 2007 with its 250MB memory, expandable by SD card and started at the price of 400usd. This was the first step towards establishing a global eBook market. Following the uproar of smart tablets, Amazon released the Kindle Fire, a multi-purpose e-reader capable of playing music, videos, and apps, all while still serving its original function. The Kindle Fire is a cheaper alternative than any other expensive tablets. The Kindle has a newer version of the Kindle Fire HD, now (2013) comes with storage of 16Gb, 32GB or 64GB, 20 percent faster processor and double the memory (1GB) of the original kindle while still maintaining the battery life for 8 to 10 hours.

1.7 - From all the many eBook markets, why Kindle?

Competition is high among the most popular ePublishers (Smashwords, Barns and Nobles, Kobo and Apple). Depending on the experience of each user, the choice comes with some reasons that make the user more comfortable to work with the chosen ePublisher. However, it is believed that Amazon is among the largest player in the eBook market. This means that Amazon owns the biggest portion of customers in eBooks market. For authors, this is good news because their eBooks will have more exposure and will be more likely to get readers. To top it off, Amazon is one of the largest companies in the eBook market. With immense funds and resources at their deposition, the Amazon has invested funds to keep attracting customers. Considering the annual growth the kindle market is experimenting, it is believed that Amazon's electronic book store will become the top place to buy and read all sorts of eBooks in the next 10 years.

CHAPTER II

2. - Developing and writing process

2.1 - Choose your topic

Before you begin the actual publishing process, it is time to take a step back and become an author first. Profits and money should be completely out of your mind when you are in the process of writing your book. The reason why this is so important is because money can corrupt the creative process. Readers who will buy your book will want to be informed, entertained, or both. Because this is always the case, is important to focus on developing worth reading of content. Many authors make the fatal mistake of relying on gimmicks, marketing tricks and other cheap tactics to receive sales or book downloads. Although these are some short term solutions, as an author you want to build a name and a reputation. Authors who rely on short term marketing tricks receive soon after bad reviews, negative press and will fail to make on going revenues from their work. With this said, focus on producing the best piece of content you can create.

2.2 - Writing phase

The right mindset to have when you are first developing your book is an optimistic view. Understand that you are most likely not going to become a millionaire from your first publications. Some important statistics show that during 2011 over 300,000 books were self-published. Most of these books did not become best sellers. Some of them did not even make a sale during the year. According to the famous newspaper and media outlet, The Guardian, the average income generated from eBooks to authors averaged 10,000 dollars a year. Once again, it is important to remember. It is not about the money during the writing phase. It is the creation of a product which is useful, informative and most important that can compete against the other 300,000 published books.

As you write your first draft, you should not worry so much about your delivery or editing the work, you should concentrate on finishing writing the book. You might become counter-productive in editing prior to finishing the book. Whatever is written down, it will all be edited at the end. Editing while your work is not yet done will only consume more time and will keep you from moving forward.

2.3 - Proofreading

When you finish writing your first rough draft, the first things you must do is have it checked, proofread. Investing on a professional edit will add value to your book and to your readers. In a business where credibility is everything, you do not want to lose image and reputation over grammar issues. After successfully editing your book, the next move is to take the legal steps towards copyrighting your content. Most conventional books also include a table of content or index that help readers find what they are looking for quick. If you feel like making an ethical reference to someone who helped you develop your book, create an acknowledgement page or perhaps even a prologue that lets the readers see the behind the scenes of your book development.

2.4 - Book cover and visual designs

When it comes to developing visuals for your book, an amazing cover should be first in your list. In the printed copy, publishers took care of this part of book development, but with self-publishing, these responsibilities fall on the shoulders of the author. Most readers judge books by their covers. A book cover is the first glimpse of a book readers get to see. It should be catchy, eye popping and perhaps even intriguing. The point is that a book cover should translate some emotions to the readers. Book cover elements are very important for fiction writers.

When it comes to book covers, you will also want a second eye to challenge your perception of the appeal of the cover. Try to find a focus group or perhaps close friends that are willing to give you an honest opinion of the look of your book cover. However, because not everyone is artistically inclined, sometimes you will simply have to go with your inner voice. Amazon requires your cover to be a high quality 800 pixels by 1066 pixels cover. Larger covers can be added, but consider the fees you might have to pay for the extra megabytes (discussed later).

More importantly, make sure your book cover transmits the same message in a 160 by 240 pixel scale. Your visitors will only get to see the full cover when they arrive at the book's main page. In reality, your book will be displayed as a 160 by 240 thumbnail in "related books" and book lists.

Graphic designs can be a major expense. Good, quality graphics do not come cheap and are usually done by professionals. A freelance graphic designer can charge anywhere from 99 to 400 dollars to design a well-made book cover.

Graphic designers will add that extra layer of professionalism that only a professionally made book cover can bring. The price of your cover will depend on various factors. The first factor is the expertise of the graphic designer. The more professional and client oriented your graphic designer is, the more he charges you, but he will produce a high quality end product. The price of your design will also depend on the amount of time a designer believes completing your cover will require. Personalized graphics and high definition cartoons/illustration can be more time consuming than a light Photoshop job. Lastly, your price will depend greatly on the reputation of the graphic designer or the company. You can find considerably cheaper work done by professional designers who have yet to establish themselves and are starting their career. The only problem is that, because they lack the vouchers and reputation that established designers have, it might be a riskier deal. Weight your options and see which sort of graphic designer you wish to work on your book cover.

2.5 - Copyright information

Once your book has been finished and has been published under a name, is considered by the US law "in fixed tangible form" and thus is copyrighted. Because this concept might be hard to grasp, and some of us truly want to avoid any loopholes in the system, you might be interested in reading a guide by Mediashift on how to copyright your digital book for no more than 40 dollars.

CHAPTER III

3. - Formatting and publishing your eBook

Self-publishing in Amazon is a rather technical matter. The process occurs as an electronic walk that allows you to publish your book online, much like you would when uploading a video to the net.

3.1 - File size and fees

In the process of finally publishing your first book, you will discover that file size affects the "delivery fee". In essence, Amazon hosts your book file and must "use" bandwidth every time someone downloads your digital book. Bandwidth can be very expensive at the scale of Amazon's enterprise. For this reason as part of their business model, Amazon added a "delivery fee" that is charged every time someone downloads your eBook. This delivery fee also includes an extra percentage that accounts as the royalties' Amazon will take from your book as profit. To summarize, the larger your book, the higher the deliver fee will be.

3.2 - Converting word file into HTML

Some ways to successfully reducing the size of the fee is converting your word file, into a simple "code dense" format. The simplest format available (that Kindle is able to process) is html. A problem you will face by converting your word eBook into plain html code will most likely revolve around unnecessary code appearing in the simpler html file. The reason why this occurs is that the word is a more sophisticated program with some codes that are often unreadable in html. To solve part of this problem, simply save the word document as a "web page filtered" document. This will clean most of the unnecessary codes that are transferred through regular conversion. The main structure of html will always appear like this:

```
<!DOCTYPE html PUBLIC "-//W3C//DTD HTML 4.01
Transitional//EN">
<html>
<head>
<meta content-"text/html; charset=ISO-8859-1" http-
equiv="content-type">
<title></title>
</head>
<body>
<br>
</body>
</html>
```

By converting the word file into "web page filtered", you will eliminate most of the unnecessary code. However, you will still have to format the eBook in order to make it more enjoyable to readers. Follow some of these tips to improve the readability of your eBook. Some of these tips require basic coding knowledge. In order to put these tips into function, you will have to manually input the code into the html file.

3.3 - Create page brakes

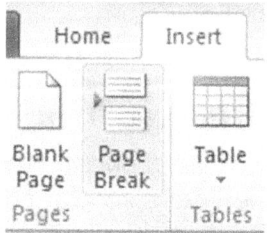

Create page breaks at the end of every chapter. That is the way your Kindle will read the page starting from new for a new chapter. Showing and hiding the sign [¶] will help when typing to locate the marking. Header, footer page are not necessary in Kindle as the reading of the text is not in fixed page.

3.4 - Check your scene breaks.

Occasionally, depending on your version of the word or text program, when converting your eBook into an html, the code indicating a break can be lost. To fix this problem, go into your html file and add a hash character (#) followed by a unique character to mark a scene break. In html syntax code, it indicates a comment which is not printed out on the browser.

```
if 1900 < year < 2100 and 1 <= month <= 12 \
    and 1 <= day <= 31 and 0 <= hour < 24 \
    and 0 <= minute < 60 and 0 <= second < 60:    # - Here is
a comment -
        return 1
```

3.5 - Check for basic html coding.

Remember that your text editing follows basic html code in order to display the pages of your eBook. Look for consistency and add or replace any code that might be missing. A good example is to make sure your paragraphs have the "<p>...</p>" tags at the beginning and at the end of every complete paragraph.

Luckily for most authors, the Kindle previewing software allows you to have a good look of your book before it is actually published. Websites for software tools are given at the end of the book. A good idea is to check every page of your book and make sure it is readable and clear of any coding mistakes. Note that, as software, it has its limitations. Links are not visible in the Kindle preview software; thus it is important to correct any mistakes that might come up after the actual publishing. For graphic oriented books, "Format 8" allows publishers to create HTML5 and CSS savvy book pages that are highly responsive and exciting for readers. Format 8 also allows you to convert your word file directly into a Kindle file.

3.6 - Setting up book with images

If you don't use any pictures or images in your book, you can ignore this step. If you use images, you have to compress them in a ZIP file to make them working with Kindle. Logos, reference images and other graphics are supported by Kindle e-Reading format. Insert the images during typing instead of copy-paste them. Do not simply wrap the images around text as an attempt to embed them in with inline format. Naturally when you convert a word file into html, a special folder is created to hold all of the graphics. If the name of your document is `eBook.doc`, a folder "eBook_files" will be automatically created to hold the pictures. Before uploading your eBook into Amazon, extract all the images from the folder and place them in the same folder as your html book. Then you will have manually to edit the html code so that all the images point to the right places. Notepad++ (cf. Appendix - Software Tools) is a simple text-editor you can use for manual edit the html.

A good way to do this is to run the search function in your html code file, and look for "eBook_files/" then delete all of "eBook_files/" names in the html file. It means the pictures are no longer in the folder but together at the same place as the html file. For example, the code in your html might be pointing to

"img width="275" height="135" src="eBook_files/image001.jpg" alt="first image", but since the images are no longer in the folder, you will have to change the code to "img width="275" height="135" src="eBook_files/image001.jpg" alt="first image", otherwise the images will not appear on your book.

You take the images from inside the folder "eBook_files" to be at the same level of "eBook.html". Once you have formatted all the images to point to the right locations, convert your document into a zip file. Zip all images and the "eBook.html" in one file called "eBook.zip". This compressed version of your eBook will be the file to be uploaded to Amazon. Do not worry about computability, Amazon will decompress and read your eBook perfectly. It is important to make sure not to upload your cover image into the zip document as this image goes somewhere else. If you are not sure of which editing format to use, ask for professional help.

3.7 - Indent-paragraphs

To create indent-paragraphs, do not use Tab or Space. To indent paragraph on the first line, click on the top menu "Page Layout" and then find "Paragraph" section. At the right corner, click the downward arrow which will show:

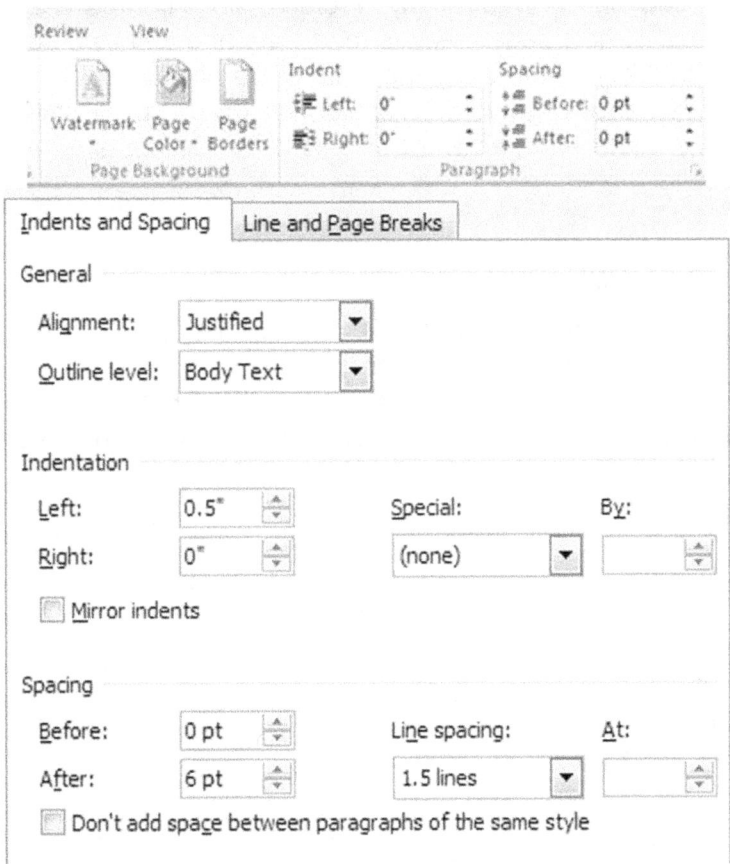

3.8- Space in between paragraphs

Instead of using "Return" to create lines between two paragraphs, go to "Indents and Spacing" as shown in the "Page Layout" top menu in the word document.

Spacing

			Line spacing:	At:
Before:	0 pt			
After:	6 pt		1.5 lines	

☐ Don't add space between paragraphs of the same style

Title, Copyright, Dedication, Preface are printed each in separated pages, page break is the formatting tool to be used in the separating them during the editing. Do not use Tab or Space to put sentence or a word centered. Use the word document tab menu to make centered word or phrases. Headings are readable for Kindle.

3.9 - Table of Contents

Table of contents in Kindle are like hyper-links, when clicking the link, it directs the reader to the location of the content. Kindle can read the Table of Contents you create with Microsoft Word. Set the Headings to format the Table of Contents if not yet done.

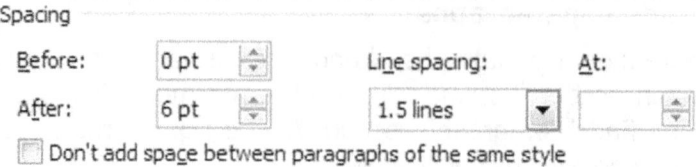

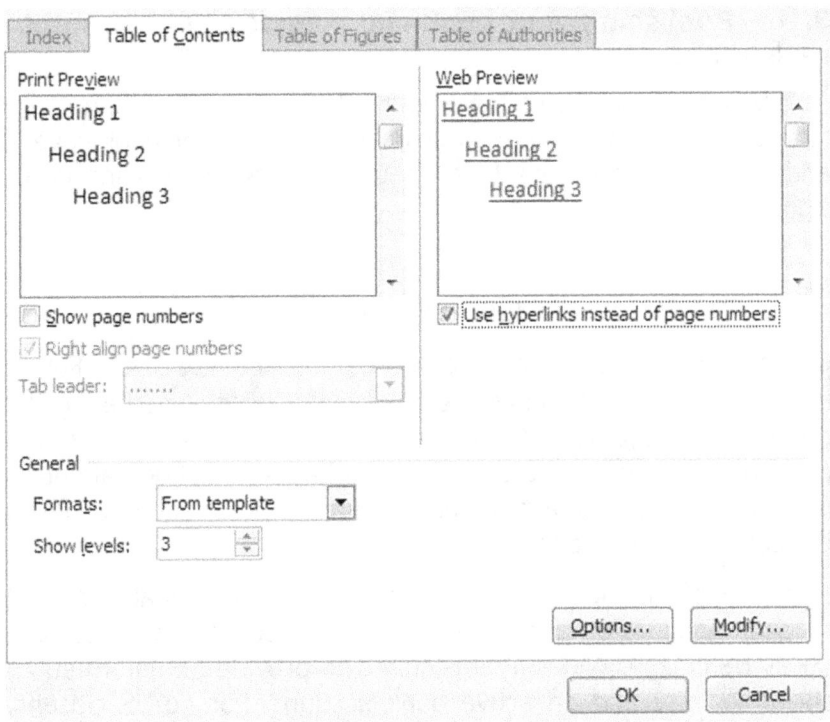

Click on "Table of Contents" icon, scroll down to find at the bottom of the menu "Insert Table of Contents". Uncheck the "Show Page Numbers" and fix "Show levels" box to 1 and then click "OK". There is called "Guide Items" in Kindle to locate a passage from anywhere within the content. To create it, set a bookmark to direct Kindle to locate your Table of Contents. Cover, introduction and chapters can be found by Kindle through bookmarks as "Guide Items". To fix your Table of Contents as a "Guide Item", do these: highlight the "Table of Contents", click "Insert" tab menu, take "Bookmark" and in the "Bookmark name", write "TOC" (no quote marks) then click "Add".

3.10 - Publishing your book and completing your author registration

At this point, you should have your eBook compressed into a zip file. It should contain all of your images (except for book cover), and an edited html book text. To upload, start by signing up or signing in to KDP select.

http://kdp.amazon.com/

Go to "Bookshelf" and click on "Add new title". Follow the instructions and you will be asked to complete the field (title, description, royalties, categories, etc.). Make a well written description to portrait to the readers what is your book about. It is from your metadata that readers may be introduced to know the content of your book.

In the application, you can either use your personal shopping Amazon Account or create a new one altogether. When you sign up as US citizen, you will be required to provide tax information, social security and an active bank account. For no-US citizens, just follow the instructions during the sign up. Needless to say, part of this information is used to discount a percentage of the revenue you make to pay for your taxes. This information is also used by Amazon to prevent any sort of fraud and verify the authenticity of your identity in real life. With your account information in place, Amazon will now be able to pay you royalties. The minimum money threshold is 10 dollars. This means that you need to make at least this much money before Amazon sends you this money electronically.

Once you have provided this information, the registration will be completed. You will be redirected to the "KDP Bookshelf" which shows the books you have previously published under that account name. Click the "add new" button and upload your book file.

Talking again about the description, remember that the book description is the next point, after the title and cover page, readers will use to decide whether or not to download your book.

Make it interesting and possibly even dedicate some time to brainstorm an eye catching book description but not exaggerated.

Lastly, add book title, add to whether or not to enroll your book in the lending program (KDP book select), give your book categories, select or create a book series, and lastly decide whether or not to enable Digital Rights Management, more on this below. When your book is uploaded in KDP, you can do the preview to see how the book will be displayed on Kindle devices, and other applications (apps), and then go ahead and advance to the next step.

3.11 - Digital Rights Management

DRM for short was introduced to amazon to help publishers "regulate" copyrights and sharing laws. DRM, when enable, makes to harder for individuals to counterfeit your book. However, this option is often not recommended as it also affects regular readers who try and share the book with family and friends. Even though the choice is yours, it is recommended to new authors not to enable this option as is permanent.

3.12 - Pricing and exclusivity rights

Naturally you will receive a 70 percent royalty for every book that is sold. The minimum price of your book is $2.99 and the maximum is $9.99. Of course if your book is part of the lending program, you will be giving exclusivity to Amazon for 90 days and you will not be able to sell the book anywhere else, but even then the price cannot go below 99 cents.

The lending program might not seem as the best choice revenue wise, but the program has a monthly pool of over 6 million dollars that is shared among all the authors that participate in the program. When entering your book into the lending program, remember to click on the option that ends the exclusivity agreement at the 90 days mark. If this option is not selected,

Amazon will simply renew the "contract' once the 90 days are up. Even though the agreement stays 90 days, you can remove your book from the lending program at any time.

In the second step of your book publishing you will have to select the geographical territories you wish for your book to appear. Most English books that cover very specific topics are sold globally. Niche books that may discuss a specific topic and/or are written in a different language can be sold in specific locations. From the 246 specify the places you want to sell the book, if you want to sell the book globally, select that option. At the time comes to delivery fee, double check the weight of the file. If your book includes very little graphics and your file size surpasses 1MB, maybe you will want to cancel the publishing and reedit your file in a way that you assure you are paying the lowest delivery cost.

You will be able to decide whether or not to enter the lending program one last time on the second step. If you have made your choice it is time to click "save and publish". Within 12 hours, Amazon will receive your book and put it live on the marketplace. Download your own book and make sure all the pages make sense and all the graphics are in place. If you find any particular mistake, you can also re-upload the file and make the adequate corrections to your book.

The eBook industry is now growing as the physical book sales slowly decline. This is a true testament of the eBooks power affecting the publishing industry in the years to come. Publishing your first book as an author is a great way of getting early on a growing market. Nevertheless book publishing requires more than just uploading your book into Amazon. With over 300,000 books published a year, you will have to market your book in order to gain popularity and most importantly drive sales. If you want to reap the revenues and royalties that come from becoming a successful self-published author you will have to put even more work towards marketing your product .Promoting your eBook can be tricky, for this reason in the next chapter it will be shared some of the most effective and creative ways of promotion your new book.

CHAPTER IV

4. - Promoting your eBook

Before we discuss marketing strategies, is important to understand that marketing can be the hardest part of your publishing career. Authors who dive into marketing must do two things; the first is to be as creative as possible, and the second is to be organized and strategic. The reason many new books fail to reach their costumers is because the authors did not approach their book publishing as a business. Understand that your book is your product, and somewhere out there your market is interested on your book. You need to find ways to reach this public and get their attention. Of course, this is easier said than done.

Many authors fail to even designate a budget, or at least draw a plan of how they will tackle the marketing of their products. No business or story will be heard without proper marketing and so is important to have a very detailed plan of your marketing. Investing the time to research and get informed as to how effective marketing looks like can be valuable. Take some time to understand your audience and what their interests are. If you are serious about making book sales, you will most likely need to market your book.

4.1 - Web marketing strategies

4.1.1 - Build a website

Needless to say, presentation is fundamental for any business. You will probably never buy from a shady store that has broken windows and dirty merchandise. Pay attention to your store, which is your site. Have it designed by a professional if you may. A professional website follows a consistent theme. If it is possible, make your website have same color patterns as your eBook. Don't forget to add quality writing on your site to engage all the visitors that arrive at your website.

Focus on simplicity. Visitors want to be led directly to reach what they are looking for on your site. Tell a story of your book, and ultimately attempt to add exits to your site that lead to buying or downloading.

4.1.2 - Testimonies and reviews sell for themselves

How many times have you been faced with a product that seemed really good, yet you did not buy it for lack of trust. Reviews influence 87% of sales[3]. Give away copies of your book in exchange for some real credible reviews of your product. Then, add some of these reviews to your site. Internet companies have to rely on authority. Let potential readers know that others have tried your product with customer testimonies.

4.1.3 - Use keywords in your Domain Name

It is very tempting for new authors to use their pen name as their domain name. The problem with this is that if you lack credibility and recognition, your name does not mean much. Work on making sales and promoting your product first. Once you start having a trail of success you can be free to start a real site using your pen name, until then focus on finding keywords your potential readers look for and build a site (or sites) that focus on these keywords.

4.1.4 - Use video marketing

Youtube is the second largest search engine in the world, and that is for one reason alone; everyone responds to video presentations and visuals. Do not let the video marketing opportunity to pass by you. Invest some money and preferably time, in creating videos that your target audience is looking for and then remind them of your book at the end. Make, if you may, promotional videos, useful video content that attempt to solve a problem for your readers.

4.1.5 - Get busy in Social Networks

The value of social network for business making is nothing than the people talking about your product. Facebook, Twitter and other social sites are now the top for business companies or individuals to advertise their products. This marketing strategy allows every visitor to know your book and also to spread the word about your products.

4.1.6 - Use Press Releases

Online fresh press releases news can circle the internet faster without the need of ranking your site or any other long term work. You have written an exciting book that most likely helps people in one way or another. Prepare a press release that announces your creativity to create an excitement of interest in your book. Many press releases services will distribute your news headlines for a fee. This may not sound favorable, but press releases work exceptionally for eBooks. Take some time to create an interesting press release that focuses on something interesting about your eBook and concept. If your press release reaches the audience you can expect buzz and even sales/downloads.

4.2 - Promotional marketing

Giving away things for free are hardly ever understood. It might be difficult to see the value of free promotions but remember that big companies in all industry have free promotions. This is because it works. Something you have to give in order to receive and that is what marketing is all about. It is true that not every user that gains something free from your promotion will share or add value to your efforts. But those users who take the extra step and spread the word, add reviews online and do free media for you are all worthy.

4.2.1 - Give away a whole chapter

It would be good to share this much content. In fact if by the end of the chapter the person is not interested on your book they probably were not part of your target audience. However, users who are interested on the topic of your book will only need one chapter to decide whether to fly or buy. See the chapter as a marketing tool. Only 20 pages of your content will spark the interest of your readers with you having to do anything else. Readers are becoming more and more careful. They want to know what they are buying before they ever hand you their information or money. Give them the test drive they want by sharing a whole chapter.

4.2.2 - Create a contest

Contests are fun and have a double purpose. First, contests can be a great excuse to create press releases and buzz, and second of all, contests can drive sales if done correctly. You can offer a free chapter or limited copies of your book for free to the participants. You might be wondering how can this possibly help you drive sales, and the answer is the following. The first way to make a contest like these work for you is requiring participants to review your book after they have "won" you contest. You will gain ratings from all of these free reviewers. The second way to drive sales with contests is to offer chapters and ask for either reviews and/or a link to buy the whole book. When you offer chapters for free but valuable information, users who are genuinely interested will pursue your book and even buy the whole version. Coordinate your contest well in advance and figure out exactly what you will want to get out of the participants.

4.2.3 - Give away bonus content

It is understandable if you do not want to reward non buyers but you reserve bonus content for paid readers. If this is the case, creating special bonus content can be the way to go. Bonus content sounds exciting as well as intriguing to potential readers.

If you offer bonus content for free at your site and at the end/beginning of every excerpt you show a link pointing to the actual book. Interested readers will follow your content and eventually buy it if they feel it is good enough.

CONCLUSION

Now is the time, self-publish today. The book industry is undergoing a colossal change. Long gone are the days that big publishing companies had the last saying on whether or not your book would make it into the book industry. Today, Amazon's new program has allowed thousands of authors to take charge of their book's future. To top it off, every day, the price of shipping and printing a physical book are becoming more expensive and less profitable for authors and companies. Do not be fooled by the old stigma that self-published books are less likely to become best sellers. In today's electronic market, more and more good sellers are originating from authors who have taken it upon themselves to publish their own books. With Kindle becoming more and more prominent and standard eBook platform, learning how to self-publish your book can be very valuable.

The process can be overwhelming. Nevertheless, those who manage to hang on persevere and keep trying, can now call themselves accomplished authors. To those who are still struggling, look for inspiration in stores like these:

Forbes, 2012, Dec. 3, Jeremy Greenfield, "When Self-Published EBooks Become Best-Sellers",

> *«What isn't as clear is what publishers do in a world where anyone can be published as a best-seller. One of the interesting trends in the eBook revolution is that established authors who have had long-standing relationships with large publishers have in some cases decided to abandon those publishers and go it alone. Some of them have been so successful at it that they've made more money doing it themselves than they ever did working with a large publishing house".*[4]

Stephanie Bond's "Stop the Wedding", published in November 11th 2012 by Need to Read Books has become the 6th most downloaded book in the US, middle of January 2012[5], making it a best seller. Although Stephanie's writing prowess is obvious from her early work, this is her first real break as an author. Number #2 eBook best-selling on Kindle, the romantic comedy of Stephanie Bond sells 3,500 copies per day at 99 cents per copy. In a week it makes $24,500 and $98,000 in a month.

Even big publishing companies are no longer ignoring the digital, viral power best-selling books have. One of the largest self-publishing platforms, Author Solutions, was bought by Penguin in the year 2012. A deal that cost them over 100 million dollars, but has the potential to generate many times that amount.

Some big publishing companies have seen the potential interest in buying the rights of already best-selling eBooks. Simon and Schuster, a major publisher, stroke a deal with Colleen Hoover, a best-selling eBook author, and acquired the rights to some of his work. In reality, authors who are backed up by the power of a big publisher can become best sellers selling their books for over ten dollars, while Stephanie only reaps a 10 percent of that price. However, much like all best-selling authors, Stephanie is building something perhaps more important than instant money; a loyal fan-base that will buy her work from now on."

BIBLIOGRAPHY

Amazon. *Amazon Kindle user's guide.* S.l.: Amazon.com, 2011.

Bond, Stephanie. *Stop the Wedding!* NeedtoRead Books, 2012.

Frankel, Valerie Estelle. *Free Guide to Self-Publishing and Book Promotion - Inside Secrets from an Author Whose Self-Published Books Sold in Thousands.* Smashwords Edition, 2012.

Kline, L.V. *Why Online Marketing Matters : How Small Business Can Get More Customers, Sales & Profits.* Pete's Publishing, 2012.

Kukral, Jim F. *What Is Internet Marketing? Learn from the Web's top entrepreneurs & small business owners.* Digital Book Launch, 2011.

Ponnapalli, Pardu S. *Creating a Kindle book using HTML templates.* 2012.

APPENDIX
Software Tools

"Amazon.com: **Kindle for PC** - Read Kindle eBooks on your PC." *Amazon.com: Online Shopping for Electronics, Apparel, Computers, Books, DVDs & more*. N.p., n.d. Web. 25 Jan. 2013.
<http://www.amazon.com/gp/feature.html?docId=1000426311>.

"**Kindle Previewer**." *Amazon.com: Online Shopping for Electronics, Apparel, Computers, Books, DVDs & more*. N.p., n.d. Web. 25 Jan. 2013.
<http://www.amazon.com/gp/feature.html?ie=UTF8&docId=1000765261>.

"Mobipocket.com – **Mobipocket Creator**, eBooks and ebook reader for your PC, PDA and Smartphone: Palm, Windows mobile, Symbian, Blackberry, or PocketPC.." *Mobipocket.com - eBooks and eBook reader for your PC, PDA and Smartphone: Palm, Windows mobile, Symbian, Blackberry, or PocketPC..* N.p., n.d. Web. 25 Jan. 2013.
<http://www.mobipocket.com/en/DownloadSoft/DownloadCreator.asp>.

"Notepad++ **Notepad++ 6.2.2** released." *Notepad++ Home*. N.p., n.d. Web. 25 Jan. 2013. <http://notepad-plus-plus.org/news/notepad-6.2.2-release.html>.

WEBOGRAPHY

"5 Advanced Social Media Marketing Strategies for Small
Businesses." *Mashable.* N.p., n.d. Web. 25 Jan. 2013.
<http://mashable.com/2009/09/30/small-business-
strategies/>.

"5 Ways Free Press Release Sites Can Cost You - 30 Minute PR."
Online PR Expert Marc Harty" 30 Minute PR. N.p., n.d.
Web. 25 Jan. 2013. <http://www.30minutepr.com/5-
ways-free-press-release-sites-can-cost-you/>.

"8 in 10 Americans Agree That Online Reviews Influence Their
Purchases." *MarketingCharts: charts & data for
marketers in online, Excel and PowerPoint formats.* N.p.,
n.d. Web. 26 Jan. 2013.
<http://www.marketingcharts.com/wp/topics/asia-
pacific/8-in-10-americans-agree-that-online-reviews-
influence-their-purchases-25761>.

"Amazon Best Sellers: best Kindle eBooks." *Amazon.com: Online
Shopping for Electronics, Apparel, Computers, Books,
DVDs & more.* N.p., n.d. Web. 25 Jan. 2013.
<http://www.amazon.com/Best-Sellers-Kindle-Store-
eBooks/zgbs/digital-text/154606011>.

"Amazon.com: Kindle for PC - Read Kindle eBooks on your PC."
*Amazon.com: Online Shopping for Electronics, Apparel,
Computers, Books, DVDs & more.* N.p., n.d. Web. 25
Jan. 2013.
<http://www.amazon.com/gp/feature.html?docId=1000
426311>.

"Amazon's Kindle Direct Publishing." N.P., n.d. Web 25 Jan. 2013.
<https://kdp.amazon.com/self-publishing/signin>

"Beneifts of Press Releases." *Search Engine Optimization -
Internet Marketing -SEO Optimization / SEO Inc.* N.p.,
n.d. Web. 25 Jan. 2013.
<http://www.seoinc.com/optimized-press-
releases/benefits>.

"EXCLUSIVE: Hard Numbers For Successful Free Book Sampling
On Amazon - Forbes." *Information for the World's*

Business Leaders - Forbes.com. N.p., n.d. Web. 25 Jan. 2013.
<http://www.forbes.com/sites/davidvinjamuri/2012/09/1 9/exclusive-hard-numbers-for-successful-free-book-sampling-on-amazon/>.

"How to Make Your Ebook a Run-Away Success: An Interview with Jim Kukral." *Write to Done / Unmissable articles on writing.* N.p., n.d. Web. 25 Jan. 2013.
<http://writetodone.com/2012/03/17/how-market-eBooks/>.

"Kindle Direct Publishing Adds $1.5 Million Holiday Bonus for KDP Select Authors | Business Wire." *Press Release Distribution, Financial Disclosure, Online Newsrooms, PR, Public Relations, Investor Relations, EDGAR filing, XBRL, Breaking News, Business News, Financial News / Business Wire.* N.p., n.d. Web. 25 Jan. 2013.
<http://www.businesswire.com/news/home/2012112900 5417/en/Kindle-Direct-Publishing-Adds-1.5-Million-Holiday>.

"Kindle Direct Publishing Adds $1.5 Million Holiday Bonus for KDP Select Authors| Reuters." *Business & Financial News, Breaking US & International News / Reuters.com.* N.p., n.d. Web. 25 Jan. 2013.
<http://www.reuters.com/article/2012/11/29/idUS68454 +29-Nov-2012+BW20121129>.

"Kindle Previewer." *Amazon.com: Online Shopping for Electronics, Apparel, Computers, Books, DVDs & more.* N.p., n.d. Web. 25 Jan. 2013.
<http://www.amazon.com/gp/feature.html?ie=UTF8&do cId=1000765261>.

"Mobipocket.com - eBooks and eBook reader for your PC, PDA and Smartphone: Palm, Windows mobile, Symbian, Blackberry, or PocketPC.." *Mobipocket.com - eBooks and eBook reader for your PC, PDA and Smartphone: Palm, Windows mobile, Symbian, Blackberry, or PocketPC..* N.p., n.d. Web. 25 Jan. 2013.
<http://www.mobipocket.com/en/DownloadSoft/Downlo adCreator.asp>.

"Notepad++ Notepad++ 6.2.2 released." *Notepad++ Home*.
    N.p., n.d. Web. 25 Jan. 2013. <http://notepad-plus-
    plus.org/news/notepad-6.2.2-release.html>.

Parnell, Brid-Aine. "Affected by eBook price-fixing? Amazon has a
    few shiny pennies for you - The Register." *The Register:*
    Sci/Tech News for the World. N.p., n.d. Web. 25 Jan.
    2013.
    <http://www.theregister.co.uk/2012/10/15/ebook_price_
    fixing_settlement_distribution/>.

Richardson, Andy, and CEO of Influential Software. "Have We
    Already Reached Peak E-book? | Publishing
    Perspectives." *Publishing Perspectives - International*
    publishing news & opinion. N.p., n.d. Web. 25 Jan. 2013.
    <http://publishingperspectives.com/2012/10/have-we-
    already-reached-peak-e-book/>.

"Self-published e-Book author: 'Most of my months are six-figure
    months' - CNN.com." *CNN.com - Breaking News, U.S.,*
    World, Weather, Entertainment & Video News. N.p., n.d.
    Web. 25 Jan. 2013.
    <http://www.cnn.com/2012/09/07/tech/mobile/kindle-
    direct-publish/index.html>.

"Would you rent an eBook from Amazon? - Liliputing." *Liliputing -*
    Compact Computing. N.p., n.d. Web. 25 Jan. 2013.
    <http://liliputing.com/2013/01/would-you-rent-an-
    ebook-from-amazon.html>.

NOTES

Frankel, Valerie Estelle. *Free Guide to Self-Publishing and Book Promotion - Inside Secrets from an Author Whose Self-Published Books Sold in Thousands*. Smashwords Edition, 2012.

[2]http://www.forbes.com/sites/davidvinjamuri/2012/09/19/exclusive-hard-numbers-for-successful-free-book-sampling-on-amazon

[3]http://www.marketingcharts.com/wp/topics/asia-pacific/8-in-10-americans-agree-that-online-reviews-influence-their-purchases-25761/

[4]http://www.forbes.com/sites/jeremygreenfield/2012/12/03/when-self-published-ebooks-become-best-sellers/

[5]http://www.amazon.com/Best-Sellers-Kindle-Store-eBooks/zgbs/digital-text/154606011

DEFINITION
MLA style

n.p. ("no publisher") there is no publisher's name

n.p. ("no place") there is no city of publication

n.d. ("no date) there is no publication date

N.P., n.d. Web 25 Jan. 2013., with the the URL was retrieved

Example:

"Amazon's Kindle Direct Publishing." N.P., n.d. Web 25 Jan. 2013.
https://kdp.amazon.com/self-publishing/signin

www.ingramcontent.com/pod-product-compliance
Lightning Source LLC
Chambersburg PA
CBHW051300170526
45165CB00004B/1787